HANG GLIDING

WITHDRAWN

By Noel Whittall

Gareth Stevens
Publishing

Please visit our web site at www.garethstevens.com
For a free catalog describing our list of high-quality books, call 1-800-542-2595 (USA)
or 1-800-387-3178 (Canada). Our fax: 1-877-542-2596

Library of Congress Cataloging-in-Publication Date available upon request from publisher.

ISBN-10: 0-8368-8960-6   ISBN-13: 978-0-8368-8960-4 (lib. binding)

This U.S. edition copyright © 2008 by Gareth Stevens, Inc. Original edition copyright © 2007 by ticktock Media Ltd., First published in Great Britain in 2007 by ticktock Media Ltd., Unit 2, Orchard Business Centre, North Farm Road, Tunbridge Wells, Kent, TN2 3XF

ticktock project editor: Julia Adams
ticktock project designer: Sara Greasley
ticktock picture researcher: Lizzie Knowles
editor: Ben Hubbard

Gareth Stevens Senior Managing Editor: Lisa M. Guidone
Gareth Stevens Creative Director: Lisa Donovan
Gareth Stevens Graphic Designer: Giovanni Cipolla
Gareth Stevens Associate Editor: Amanda Hudson

Picture credits (t=top; b=bottom; c=centre; l=left; r=right):
David Bagley/ Alamy: 34/35. Denis Balibouse: 48/49t, 58. Denis Balibouse/ Red Bull Photofiles: 24/25, 44/45, 48b. Bettmann/ Corbis: 10/11t. Elizabeth Czitronyi/ Alamy: 57t. Steve Elkins: 19b. Flybubble Paragliding School, www.flybubble.co.uk: 29t. Getty Images: 9t, 9b. Ulrich Grill/ Red Bull Photofiles: 31tr. John Heiney: 59b. INSADCO Photography/ Alamy: 42t. Vitek Ludvik/ Red Bull Photofiles: 28. Alfredo Martinez/ Red Bull Photofiles: 20/21. Mary Evans Picture IIbrary: 7c. Ian Mills, 10fifty.com: 15tr. Paraglidingshop.co.uk: 33t. Christian Pondella/ Red Bull Photofiles: 49b. Francois Portmann/ Red Bull Photofiles: 51c. Bill Ross/ Corbis: 29b. Pasi Salminen/Red Bull Photofiles: 51tr. Shutterstock: 1, 2, 3, 4/5, 12/13, 14t, 15cl, 16, 17t, 17b, 20b, 22, 23bl x3, 27 all, 32, 43tr, 56b, 61. Bernhard Spöttel/ Red Bull Photofiles: 46. Square1.com: 33br. The Print Collector/ Alamy: 8. Noel Whittall: 10b, 11b, 18/19, 26, 37b, 38, 39t, 39b, 40/41t, 40b, 41b, 43bl, 47t, 47b, 50t, 53br, 56t, 57c, 59t, 60. Wikipedia: 36/37t. Wingsofrogallo.org: 23tr. David Wootton: 6/7t, 17c, 30t, 33c, 52cr, 52/53t, 54/55. Tim Wright/Corbis: 36b.

Every effort has been made to trace the copyright holders for the photos used in this book, and the publisher apologizes in advance for any unintentional omissions. We would be pleased to insert the appropriate acknowledgements in any subsequent edition of this publication.

Printed in the United States of America

1 2 3 4 5 6 7 8 9 10 09 08 07

Contents

Chapter 1: First Flights   4

Free Flying 6

Early History 8

The First Gliders 10

Chapter 2: The Basics   12

How Gliders Fly 14

Controlling a Glider 16

The Hang Glider 18

The Paraglider 20

Launching and Landing 22

Chapter 3: The Gear   24

Clothing 26

Extra Protection 28

Equipment 30

Safety 32

Chapter 4: Gliders   34

Types of Hang Gliders 36

The Swift 38

Rigids 40

Types of Paragliders 42

Chapter 5: Competition   44

Glider Contests 46

Aerobatics 48

Speed Flying 50

Breaking the Record 52

Chapter 6: People and Places   54

Seven Mountains, Seven Continents 56

Amazing Stunts 58

Noel Whittall 60

Glossary 62

Index 64

chapter 1: first flights

Gliding is one of the most extreme sports out there. Fans of the sport say that it is the ultimate rush. Running off a cliff and feeling the wind pick up your glider – it's a one-of-a-kind thrill, unmatched by any other experience.

The earliest recorded attempt at flying was made in China and dates back to A.D. 559. For hundreds of years, flying remained a dream. Many people were injured and even killed trying.

There were many attempts to perform unpowered flight. Some people tried to make flapping wings to imitate birds' flight, but they lacked the power to flap them. Others tied themselves to kites but couldn't control them. Then, in the 19th century, experimenters studied the flight of gliding birds like the albatross. These birds rarely need to flap their wings. The secrets of flying began to be unlocked by people such as Otto Lilienthal and Octave Chanute.

Hang gliders and paragliders are completely unpowered. They fly in the same way as gliding birds do.

Modern hang gliding started in the 1960s, when the right combination of material and knowledge came together. People created simple gliders that could be launched on foot. Paragliders followed in the 1980s. The main difference between hang gliders and paragliders is that hang gliders have wings and a stiff framework, whereas paragliders are completely soft, like parachutes. However, they are both so light that they can easily be carried by one person.

An early attempt at flying. In 1678, Le Besnier of France managed to cross a river with his flapping paddles.

The French name for these sports is "le vol libre." The English translation is "free flight." That is just what it is all about — flying free, without an engine and without noise.

Hang gliding pioneer Otto Lilienthal conducted many test flights and suffered many injuries while developing the first hang glider.

Otto Lilienthal

The first great hang glider pilot was Otto Lilienthal. He was a German inventor who made wings out of wood and canvas in the 1880s. Otto hung by his armpits in his glider and gained some control by swinging his legs, but it was not always enough. Otto died of a fractured spine in a glider crash in 1893. By then, he had made about 2,000 flights. His studies inspired the invention of the powered airplane, a few years later.

Octave Chanute

Octave Chanute was born in France but made a fortune in the United States as an engineer, designing railroads and stockyards. Like many before him, he dreamed of flight. He built a biplane glider that his assistant tested on sand dunes along the shore of Lake Michigan, near Chicago, in 1896. The pilot hung by his armpits – just like Lilienthal – so control of the glider was difficult.

After three years of experimenting with large gliders, the Wright brothers built and flew the world's first successful powered aircraft in 1903.

An early Rogallo glider prepares for take-off.

Francis Rogallo

In the 1950s, American scientist Francis Rogallo was working in the space industry developing parachutes for spacecraft. His ideas would be adapted by sporting fliers to form the shape that everyone now recognizes as that of a hang glider. These wings were often called "Rogallos."

Wilbur Wright watches Orville Wright pilot the first successful flight in the Wright Flyer at Kitty Hawk, North Carolina, in 1903.

An early ram-air parachute

The Paraglider

From time-to-time people tried gliding with parachutes, but true success with this did not come until 1978. A group of French men began flying a new invention, ram-air parachutes, from steep mountains in the French Alps. Their original idea was to practice for parachuting competitions without paying to hire a plane to jump from. But it turned out that flying off of mountains was thrilling and fun! Soon manufacturers started making more efficient canopies designed just for gliding — and the paraglider was born.

Ram-air Airfoil canopy that is sub-divided into separate cells. The entire canopy is open at the front and closed at the back, so it is literally rammed full of air and becomes a solid flying wing.

chapter 2: the basics

Hang gliders are usually launched by running off a hill or a mountain. They can also be towed into the air by an ultralight tug aircraft. Within minutes, they can be flying at heights of up to 15,000 feet (4,500 meters)!

leading edge

Even with no engine, a glider can fly for hours. In still air, the pull of gravity causes a glider to sink. But rising air (also called lift) works against the effects of gravity. So when glider pilots find rising air, they stay airborne.

The large wing of a glider generates the lift it needs to fly by keeping the front edge (the leading edge) tilted up higher than the back (the trailing edge) as it moves forward. Gliders don't have engines to push them forward, but this tilt causes air to be deflected downward. The wing reacts by trying to rise – as if it were being propelled.

trailing edge

Staying Up

A glider keeps the air passing over its wings at just the right speed by going downhill all the time. If you see a hang glider or paraglider climbing upward, it is because the air in that part of the sky is moving upward faster than gravity is making the glider sink.

There are three types of natural lift:

Ridge lift: Ridge lift occurs when wind meets a ridge or hill and is forced upward. Pilots try to launch into this ridge lift, as it will help them climb quickly. Ridge lift rarely lasts more than twice the height of the ridge.

Thermal lift: Thermals are patches of air that have been made extra warm by the sun. Hot air rises, and thermals are often powerful enough to take gliders up to the clouds.

Wave lift: Wave lift is similar to ridge lift, but it extends much higher. It happens when wind flows down the back of one hill and is "bounced" up again when it meets the front of the next one. This can give smooth, powerful lift that may go thousands of feet into the sky.

15

From hang gliders to jumbo jets, all aircraft use three basic control movements: roll, pitch, and yaw. On most hang gliders, pilots create these movements by swinging their bodies. This process is called weight-shift control.

Roll

Roll means tilting one wing lower than the other. Pilots do this by shifting their bodies sideways. Rolling automatically causes a turn in the direction of the lower wing.

Pitch

Pitch means tilting the front of the glider up or down. This movement controls the airspeed. Pulling the body forward lowers the front, making the glider speed up. Push back, and the glider slows down.

Yaw

Yaw means moving one side of the glider forward, causing the glider to turn. When the right-hand side of the glider is moved forward, the glider moves to the left. In hang gliding, yaw is less important than in paragliding. Rolling is a far more effective way of turning a hang glider.

This paraglider is taking a left-hand turn by bringing forward the right-hand side of the canopy.

Batten

Wing

This is the basic set-up of a hang glider.

Control Frame

Control Bar

The **wing** material fits over the main frame. This material, called the sail, is made from heavy-grade nylon or Dacron. Several ribs, called **battens**, fit into long pockets sewn into each side of the wing. They keep it in the correct airfoil shape.

The **keel** runs along the length of the main frame and forms a skeleton for the glider. The **control frame** is attached to the keel and joined to the main frame with steel wires. The pilot uses the frame's **control bar** to control the movements that determine speed and direction.

Hang Point

Carabiner

Keel

Harness

The **hang point** is a strong webbing loop on the keel at the center of the control frame.

The **harness** joins to the hang point with a **carabiner**. The carabiner carries all the pilot's weight, so it has to be very strong. Harnesses are designed so that the pilot can stand up for take-offs and landings and lie flat during flight.

Quick-release catches make the glider easy to assemble for flight. The glider can be folded into a roll that can be carried on a car roof.

19

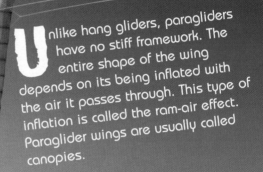

www.intellisite.ch
the new generation of websites

Unlike hang gliders, paragliders have no stiff framework. The entire shape of the wing depends on its being inflated with the air it passes through. This type of inflation is called the ram-air effect. Paraglider wings are usually called canopies.

Canopy

cell

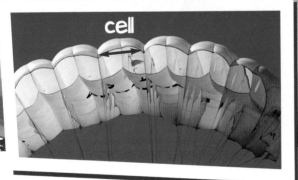

The **canopy** material is made of light, airtight nylon. The canopy itself is built up from a large number of **cells** that are sewn together side by side. Each cell is open at the front, allowing it to fill with air as the canopy flies forward.

The pilot sits in a **harness** that is joined to the canopy by many lines. These lines are carefully positioned so that when the canopy takes the weight of the pilot, it remains in the perfect shape to provide lift.

Control lines (Brakes)

Carabiners

Risers

Harness

The lines group together close to the pilot and are joined to short strips of webbing called **risers**. Small **carabiners** link these risers to both the wires and the harness.

In addition to the lines that suspend the pilot, an extra pair runs from the trailing edge of each side of the canopy to handles in front of the risers. These are the **control lines**, and they are usually referred to as **brakes**. The brakes can be used individually to help the pilot to turn the canopy.

21

Paragliders fly at a slower speed than hang gliders. Controlling a paraglider in the air is very simple. To cruise, the brake handles are held about level with the pilot's shoulders – this gives the trim speed. Raising both handles upward increases speed slightly, and pulling them both down reduces speed.

Hang glider pilots control the glider by shifting their weight to the side they wish to steer toward. In addition to steering, both types of glider are very challenging to handle. It takes a lot of training to control them. Launching and landing can be especially tricky.

A paraglider demonstrates a roll. Some display pilots use smoke flares to mark their movements in the sky.

Trim speed Speed the glider flies at if the pilot is not putting any effort into the controls

Landing

Landing a hang glider needs precise timing. Careful pilots first slow the wing by gently pushing the bar out. Next, they move their hands to the sides of the control frame to slow the glider down as it reaches the ground.

Launching

The most tricky part of paragliding is launching. If you watch skilled pilots, you will see that they first arrange the wing neatly on the ground. They then pull on some of the lines to let air into the cells and start shaping the wing. Next, they pull both the risers evenly so the wing rises above them like a giant kite. They don't start the short run into the wind to take off until the canopy is overhead and they have checked to be sure it is fully inflated.

23

chapter 3: the gear

Gliding sports are dangerous, and sometimes accidents cannot be avoided. But with the right gear, pilots can limit the danger. It is essential that pilots have the correct equipment to help them stay safe in the sky.

Hang glider and paraglider pilots must dress for high-altitude conditions. It may be warm on the ground, but in the air gliders will fly at speeds of up to 90 miles (145 kilometers) per hour. They will feel a constant windchill effect.

High Climbers

Hangliders and paragliders climb as high as the clouds on a good day. The higher they go, the colder the air becomes. Gliders can reach 15,000 feet (4,500 m). At this height, temperatures are an average of 1.9° F (-16.7°C).

Helmet

A helmet is a must. Head injuries can be life-threatening. It is easy to misjudge a landing on rough ground. For high flights, a balaclava is worn under the helmet to keep the head and neck warm. Competition pilots wear streamlined helmets to reduce drag (see image at left).

Goggles

Close-fitting sunglasses or goggles are essential because eye-damaging ultraviolet (UV) rays in sunlight are much stronger at high altitudes. Pilots choose types that make the clouds more visible. Often these have orange lenses.

Flying Suit

A one-piece flying suit is often worn for paragliding. Hang glider pilots, who fly in warm streamlined harnesses with only their heads and shoulders sticking out, often just wear jeans and windproof jackets.

P ilots are exposed to particularly tough conditions. They face harmful rays from the Sun, extremely low temperatures, and high winds. These conditions call for some additional equipment to make the flight as comfortable as possible.

Speed Arms

Anything flapping in the high winds makes for extra drag and reduced flying speeds. When speed is of the essence, pilots wear elastic Lycra sleeves over their flying suits to keep the drag from their bodies to a minimum.

Warm Hands and Feet

Keeping the hands and feet warm on a long, high flight is a serious concern for paraglider pilots. Ski gloves or mitts are usually worn for all-weather flying. Even on warm days, pilots will wear thin leather gloves for protection. Without them, it is easy to injure their fingers on the control lines. Hang glider pilots have less of a problem. Some wear thick gloves, but many prefer mitts that are fitted to the control bar. Feet need to be protected by good boots, so paragliders wear specially designed lightweight boots that give lots of ankle support.

Sun Protection

Even if the air feels cool on top of a mountain or on a glider, there is risk of sunburn. The dangerous UV rays in sunlight are much stronger at extreme heights. In addition to wearing goggles or sunglasses to protect the eyes, it is essential to use strong sunscreen to avoid severe sunburns.

In order to avoid ending up lost or sailing over dangerous terrain, glider pilots carry many gadgets and instruments with them.

Altimeter, variometer, and GPS

In a hang glider, the control frame functions as the pilot's cockpit. The pilot lies in the harness and has the instruments mounted on the control frame, where they are easy to see. Paraglider pilots have their instruments fitted into a waist-pack that is clipped to the harness and rests on their thighs in flight.

Altimeter/Vario/GPS A few years ago, these were all separate instruments. Now it is common for the altimeter, vario, and GPS to be combined into a single small case not much bigger than a cell phone.

GPS

Combined
Vario/Altimeter

A paraglider's cockpit is
attached to his or her harness.

A list of equipment a pilot will take on a flight:

Altimeter, to show the height at which the glider is currently flying.

Variometer (usually called just "vario"), to show how fast a glider is climbing or sinking. It can be dangerous to rise too quickly or too high. Oxygen levels decrease at high altitudes, and pilots can pass out before they realize they are in danger. They need oxygen equipment if they are going to fly above 12,000 feet (3,650 m).

GPS, to show and record the glider's route.

Two-way radio, in case the pilot is in danger and needs to send out an emergency signal.

In addition to the instruments shown here, a pilot's cockpit should include a holder for a special map that shows airports and routes called "airways." These "sky roads" are reserved for airliners and other powered planes. It is important that hang glider and paraglider pilots keep clear of these parts of the sky.

31

Exposure to the weather, unpredictable thermals, and wind currents have led to many accidents for gliders. Because there are so many conditions that a pilot cannot control, most carry a rescue parachute fitted to their harness.

The rescue parachute is joined to the glider by a strong line called a strop. The glider and the pilot come down together under the rescue parachute. There is no way of steering, so rescue parachutes are only used in a real emergency, such as a mid-air collision or a collapsed canopy.

When the canopy of a paraglider collapses and becomes badly tangled, there is no way of landing safely without a rescue parachute.

Landing Protection

Landings can go wrong for different reasons. A paraglider pilot may, for example, be forced to land in rough air or touch down on dangerous terrain. To protect the pilot, paragliding harnesses have built-in safety features. One of the most basic is a thick layer of plastic foam fitted down the back and under the seat of the harness to protect the pilot's spine.

Spine protection is built into the back.

A paragliding harness with a built-in airbag and extra spine protection.

Whatever type of protection is fitted into their equipment, glider pilots are taught to keep their feet together and knees bent, as the landing impact can cause serious injuries. In woodland areas, glider pilots carry a long cord in their harness to help them climb down if they land in a tree! They also carry a special knife to cut away the reserve parachute if they land in high winds and are dragged by the parachute.

Some pilots use special knives that have protected blades so they don't injure themselves.

Both hang gliders and paragliders have come a long way since manufacturers started producing them for sport in the 1970s. Today, there are types of gliders that cater to the needs of competition professionals and beginners alike.

Training gliders have fairly loose sails, so they fly slowly and are much easier to handle than competition gliders. Students on their early flights are kept close to the ground by instructors using rope tethers. Once they are used to the feel of the glider, the ropes are removed and solo flight begins.

The most basic distinction among hang gliders is between training and competition gliders. Both are controlled in exactly the same way, but competition gliders are designed to have higher top speeds. All parts of a competition glider are streamlined – including its pilot! The glider's frame is very stiff in order to keep the sail taut at speeds of up to 90 miles (145 km) per hour.

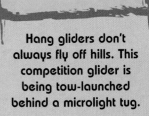

Hang gliders don't always fly off hills. This competition glider is being tow-launched behind a microlight tug.

In competitions, the usual goal is to fly a route across country as quickly as possible.
The route may be 100 miles (160 km) or more. Pilots have to find as many areas of rising air (lift) as they can to take them along the course. Unfortunately, there is always sink between patches of lift.

A fast glide is the best way to spend as little time as possible in sinking air between lifts. A very stiff wing is fastest, but it is difficult to turn. Pilots use a cord to loosen it a little.

The stiffer the wing, the faster the glider. Only experienced pilots can control a sophisticated competition hang glider.

The Swift

The Swift is a type of hang glider that is closely related to a sailplane. The performance of a Swift is spectacular compared to ordinary hang gliders. It can be flown slowly enough to take off and land at running speed, yet it has a top flying speed of about 75 miles (120 km) per hour. At its most efficient gliding speed, it sinks only 1 foot (0.3 m) for every 26 feet (8 m) that it flies forward. That's about twice as good as an average hang glider and three times as good as a paraglider. In order to achieve this, a Swift has extremely stiff wings and movable flaps on the wings to steer it, like a plane.

Swift pilots sit in built-in cockpits with door flaps in the bottom. Swifts can be launched like other hang gliders, but as soon as they are off the ground the pilots pull their legs up, close the door flaps, and relax in a seat. They control the flight with small movements of a joystick mounted on the side of the cockpit frame.

Swifts perform better than almost any other hang gliders, but they are not as easy to carry. The wings can be removed, but they are rigid and cannot be rolled up for storage. A Swift will fit in a big box on top of a car, but two people are needed to put the glider together and prepare it for launch. Because of this, Swifts are fairly rare, so you will be lucky if you spot one.

Spoilers

Rigids

In the early 1990s, a new type of hang glider – the rigid – came on the scene. Instead of using an aluminum frame, these gliders get their strength from a carbon fiber frame. The wings are rigid and use movable surfaces to make them turn.

Pilots of rigids hang in the same type of harness as on normal hang gliders. Moving backward or forward controls their speed in the usual way, but swinging sideways operates flaps on top of the wings called spoilers. When a spoiler lifts up, the glider starts to turn to that side. These spoilers, or in some cases even bigger flaps called "ailerons" (which operate at the trailing edges) mean that the rigids can turn with only a small amount of effort from the pilot, similar to a normal light aircraft.

Spars

Ribs

A rigid's strength comes from the long carbon-fiber spars that form the fronts of the wings. The wing ribs that fit onto the spars are also made of carbon-fiber, which is very light and very strong – perfect for aircraft. The wing covering fits tightly, but it can still be rolled up into a neat package for carrying around. The external framework is not as elaborate as that of traditional hang gliders, so there is less drag and they can glide more efficiently at up to 50 miles (80 km) per hour.

As with hang gliders, there are training paragliders and competition ones, with many sports types in between. The gliders used at training schools are slow and stable. The canopies have about 20 or 30 large cells and don't collapse easily. At the other extreme, competition gliders may have 100 smaller cells. They glide very well and are fast but are hard to fly. They can also collapse rapidly in unskilled hands.

The pilot of a high-performance paraglider must be able to sense the air pressure inside the wing at all times. In rough air, small movements of the brakes are constantly needed to prevent collapses from starting.

The canopy of a training paraglider (shown here) is made up of a small number of large cells, giving stability and allowing for slow flight.

A competition paraglider

A wing tip collapses

Competition gliders are flown only by experts at top events such as world championships. These professionals have had years of training and experience.

Features of the competition paraglider that distinguish it from the training paraglider include the following:

- The competition glider's canopy is wider and thinner.

- The canopy has many more cells – up to 100 total.

- The cells are smaller, which makes the canopy sensitive to air and movement.

- The lines are much thinner and thus offer less wind resistance.

- The pilot can pull the front of the canopy down with a foot-operated bar for more speed.

- The harness is shaped in a slight curve and the pilot lies back to cut wind resistance.

The competitors in a cross-country paragliding championship have about an hour to find good lift and gain height before the clock starts for the timed part of the task. The goal they have to reach may be 40 or 50 miles (65–80 km) away.

Competitions in both hang gliding and paragliding take place all over the world. Anyone can enter, as long as he or she is at least 16 years old.

There are several different types of contests for hang gliders and paragliders. They include cross-country racing (XC racing for short), landing accuracy (paragliders only), aerobatics – or Acro for short (mostly paragliders) – and speed flying and record breaking.

Hang gliders reach the inflatable finishing line after a speed race. These gliders can reach speeds of up to 55 miles (90 km) per hour.

Cross-country Racing

A cross-country race is the most popular type of competition for hang gliders and paragliders. A course is set by an expert on the local weather conditions. The course may be long – for hang gliders, 100 miles (160 km) is a common length. Start times are given, and the competitors must record their flights on their GPS instruments. At the end of the day, the information about each competitor's flight, such as speed and height achieved, is downloaded from the GPS to figure out each pilot's overall position.

Paragliding Accuracy Competitions

In paragliding accuracy championships, pilots have to make a stand-up landing on a target. The pilots must stand up at least until the canopy touches the ground. Hitting the spot is much harder than it looks, especially if the wind isn't steady. The pilot has to watch the target and the windsock all the way down while making tiny adjustments with the brakes. Pilots are penalized for each 0.4 inch (1.0 centimeter) they land away from the target's center.

Aerobatic (acro) flying on hang gliders or paragliders is a very special skill. Watch an expert perform a loop, and it looks easy and graceful. But if things go wrong, they can go very wrong indeed!

Acro competitions usually take place over a lake, with rescue boats at the ready. The biggest danger is that a pilot will fall into the canopy and become wrapped in it, unable to throw the rescue chute.

Pilots are scored for the difficulty of the things they do and on how good the whole program looks. There are both solo and pair classes.

Acro pilots can perform incredibly precise landings as part of their performance, like this one on a raft in the middle of a lake.

HANG GLIDING

Paragliders look spectacular when they mark their paths through the sky with smoke trails.

Each maneuver has a special name, like Wing-over, Helicopter Spin, Titanic Maneuver, or Infinity Tumble. Some are so difficult that only a few pilots in the world dare attempt them. They involve many loops and high-speed spirals. Acro canopies must be extra strong to withstand hard use.

The first Acro World Championships were held near Montreux, Switzerland, in 2005. Huge crowds watched the colorful show from the lakeside.

Paragliders are more flexible and offer a greater range of maneuvers. Paragliding acro is far more popular than hang gliding acro, which is practiced by only about one hundred people worldwide.

Othar Lawrence performs a wing-over, which is basically a "slanted" loop over one side of the canopy.

49

Speed flying in
the French Alps

Speed flying is the wildest of the free-flying sports. It is also the newest. It
is mainly a winter sport that takes place in mountain areas, such as the
Alps, in Europe. It combines backcountry skiing with high-level
paragliding.

Speed flyers wear skis and very small, specially made paragliders. The object is
to skim down mountainsides just a few feet above the ground. The canopies
have to fly fast to make enough lift, so they are usually launched by pilots on
skis. The pilots will sometimes land and cross patches of snow on the skis
before zooming up to clear rocks. This is thrilling but also very dangerous. The
canopies are small and very sensitive, so steering must be precise. A pilot who
over- or understeers may crash into a mountain face. Another danger lies in the
speed itself – the top record for which is 91 miles (146.5 km) per hour.

HANG GLIDING

Competition speed flying down the Swiss Alps

On top of the dangers posed by high speeds are those that come from backcountry skiing. The main danger comes from avalanches that could bury a pilot instantly under huge masses of snow. It really is a sport for experts only!

Since January 2007, annual speed flying championships have taken place in Les Arcs, in the French Alps. Competitors have to be both very fast and extremely precise to win.

Hang gliders occasionally fly events similar to downhill races called Speed Gliding.

Speed Gliding competitions are like a ski slalom in three dimensions. The pilot launches a glider from a ramp and races down the mountain while passing through "altitude control gates." These gates are like the flags in a slalom, but the glider must pass underneath them as well as between them. This maneuver involves flying and diving at speeds of up to 80 miles (130 km) per hour! Although the winner of these competitions is the fastest pilot, competitors also have to be very accurate when they race through the slalom.

51

All the official records for gliding are kept at the headquarters of the FAI (Fédération Aéronautique Internationale) in Switzerland. The FAI sets very strict rules, which must be followed by anyone who wants to get a record listed.

Many competitions involve breaking records. There are three main types of record: distance and out-and-return distance, speed around a course, and gain-of-height.

Record breaking takes a lot of planning. The weather must be perfect for the task. An early start is needed for distance records, when the pilot must expect to be in the air for many hours. Out-and-return and triangle courses are difficult because there will usually be a head wind on part of the course.

In 1989, at the age of 20, Rob Whittall became the youngest hang gliding world champion.

Out-and-return A flight circuit that begins and ends at the same point and includes one turning point

Course The distance between a start and a finish point, including any number of turning points

Austrian Manfred Ruhmer taking off at Seegrube in Innsbruck, Austria.

Manfred Ruhmer from Austria flew just over 435 miles (700 km) in Texas for the Class 1 hang glider record in 2006.

The women's hang glider record, 250 miles (400 km), is held by Kari Castle of the United States.

The record for the longest paraglider flight is held by Will Gadd of Canada, at 263 miles (423 km).

When attempting height records, pilots take along an oxygen supply, as the heights they rise to are oxygen-poor. The gain-of-height record for paragliders was set by Rob Whittall from England, flying in South Africa, in 1993. His gain was 14,849 feet (4,526 m) – that's almost 3 miles (4.5 km), straight up! The gain-of-height record for hang gliders is 14,249 feet (4,343 m). It was set in 1985 by American Larry Tudor in California.

Two record holders: Kari Castle and Davis Straub. Davis holds the record for rigid hang gliders (Class 5) at 407 miles (651 km).

chapter 6: people

and places

Whether it's launching from the highest mountain in the world or performing the most gravity-defying stunts, some pilots are driven to make gliding sports even more extreme.

French couple Zeb Roche and Claire Bernier, the owners of an adventure sports school in France, set their sights on the most adventurous task they could think of: to fly off the tops of the highest mountains on each of the seven continents of the world.

Zeb Roche and Claire Bernier, Mount Everest

Zeb had climbed Mount Everest when he was only 17, but already a skilled paraglider pilot. Claire was a paragliding champion, so they made a great team. It was still a huge task, however, and it took almost six years to complete. They set off in December 1996, using a two-seat paraglider, and returned to their school after each successful conquest to raise money for the next challenge. The most difficult summit was Mount Vinson in Antarctica, which is very hard to get to.

Mount Everest

Tandem Paraglider

Flying as a passenger in a two-seat paraglider – a tandem – can be a good way to experience free flight for the first time. Many vacation resorts offer this service. Zeb and Claire chose this method to paraglide from all the chosen mountaintops, as it was far more practical to only have to transport one paraglider up mountainsides.

The journey to Antarctica depended on catching a flight from the southernmost tip of Chile, with many delays due to bad weather. The highest launch was from Everest.

Continent	Mountain	Height
Asia	Mount Everest	29,030 ft (8,848 m)
South America	Aconcagua	22,830 ft (6,959 m)
North America	Mount McKinley	20,298 ft (6,187 m)
Africa	Mount Kilimanjaro	19,337 ft (5,894 m)
Europe	Mount Elbrus	18,480 ft (5,633 m)
Antarctica	Mount Vinson	16,863 ft (5,140 m)
Australia	Mount Kosciusko	7,314 ft (2,229 m)

amazing stunts

The Acro Kings

Félix and Raúl Rodríguez started paragliding in Spain in their early teens. Now they are world stars of paragliding acro, famous for their solo and pair performances.

58

Mike Küng

Austrian Mike Küng is one of the boldest and most inventive pilots in the world. As well as performing loops – thought for years to be impossible on a paraglider – Mike has perfected ways of launching from helicopters and balloons. Mike also broke the height record in 2004, when he launched from a balloon at a height of 33,136.5 feet (10,100 m) – 4,118.9 feet (1,255.4 m) higher than Mount Everest. The altitude meant that he needed an oxygen mask and was covered by over an inch (2.5 cm) of ice when launching!

Mike Küng launches himself out of a hot air balloon.

John Heiney performs a loop.

John Heiney

American John Heiney was one of the pioneers of acro hang gliding in the early 1980s. He is a four-time freestyle hang gliding champion and holds the record for the most consecutive loops with a hang glider.
In 1988, John launched from a hot air balloon and managed to perform fifty-two loops in a row!

Noel Whittall, the author of this book and father of multiple gliding champion Rob Whittall, has been hang gliding since 1973. He designed and built his first hang glider from scratch! Here he answers some of the questions he is often asked.

Do birds ever fly near when you hang glide?

Yes, quite frequently. In fact, some birds of prey will attack hang glider wings, but it never gets dangerous. Birds also play an important role, because they seek out thermals. Spotting a soaring bird indicates a good lift to a pilot.

Noel with his second hang glider in 1974 – he built it from a kit!

What happens if the wind drops?

Nothing. Gliders fly at their own speed through the air regardless of the wind. It is called their airspeed. Of course, the wind does make a difference to a glider's speed over the ground. From the ground, a paraglider flying with an airspeed of about 20 miles (30 km) per hour into a 20 miles (30 km) per hour wind will seem to be standing still. If the glider turns and has the wind behind it, it will seem to be doing 40 miles (65 km) per hour, but its airspeed will still be only 20 miles (30 km) per hour. Think about it. . . .

The mountains in the Austrian Alps are up to
12,500 feet (3,810 m) high!

What was the most scary situation for you in a hang glider?

I learned to hang glide in England, and all my flying was over low grassy slopes. Then I went to mountainous Austria with my glider. On my second flight, I found some good lift and managed to stay in it. For some time I paid more attention to my variometer than anything else. When I did eventually take a good look at my surroundings I was immediately hit by fear. I had just climbed above a whole mountain range! I was probably 12,000 feet (3,650 m) high in the air. The sense of exposure was overwhelming as I clung to the control bar for all I was worth. Although I knew I was on my usual glider, which I trusted completely, it suddenly felt unstable, as if it would fall out of the sky if I moved a muscle. After what seemed forever I realized I had to make myself take control, so I sped up and slowed down a few times, then flew a few circles, just to satisfy myself that I was in charge. Soon I was fairly relaxed again and enjoyed the rest of the forty-minute flight. But I'll never forget that first-time high!

Glossary

Acro Short for Aerobatics. The loops, spins, wing-overs, and other aerial stunts performed with a paraglider.

Ailerons Flaps fitted to the trailing edges of some hang gliders to make them turn in flight

Airfoil The shape formed between the upper and lower surfaces of an aircraft wing to help the wing develop lift

Altimeter An instrument that shows the height of the glider. Can be set to measure from take-off or from sea level.

Avalanche A very large and sudden rush of snow down a mountain that is seriously life-threatening to anyone in its way

Backcountry skiing Skiing in the entire area of a mountain outside resorts. Backcountry winter sports are extremely dangerous, as the terrain is unknown and the danger of avalanche activity is high.

Battens Stiffening ribs for hang glider wings

Brakes Paraglider control lines

Cells The individual divisions that make up a paraglider wing. Each cell has airfoil-shaped fabric walls between the top and bottom surfaces and an opening at the front to let air in as the wing moves forward.

Gliding The sport of unpowered flying that uses thermals and other forms of natural lift

GPS Global Positioning by Satellite. An instrument very similar to the units now found in many cars.

Joystick An aircraft control lever used on the Swift

Leading edge Front edge of the glider wing

Lift Rising air. Also used to describe the power generated by a wing moving through the air.

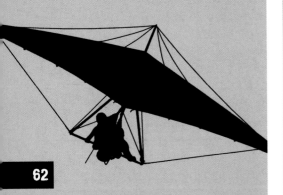

Pistes Regularly maintained slopes within a ski resort.

Ram-air effect The way a paraglider wing keeps its shape

Risers The straps between the paraglider lines and the harness

Rogallo Early hang glider named after Dr. Francis Rogallo

Rough air Air conditions, like strong winds, that make it hard to fly

Sailplane A very light aircraft that is unpowered and flies with the help of thermals

Sink Mass of air that is sinking. Gliders usually encounter them between thermals.

Slalom A race along a winding course marked by flags or poles

Spoilers Flaps on the top of a wing that "spoil" the lift to make the glider turn

Trailing edge Rear edge of a glider wing

Variometer An instrument that shows whether a glider is climbing or sinking. It is essential for all gliders, because it is impossible to tell whether you are going up or down once you are a few hundred feet above the ground.

Windchill The apparent temperature felt on the skin due to a combination of air temperature and wind speed.

Windsock A light cylinder, usually made of fabric, attached to a mast. It shows the direction and strength of the wind and is often used on airfields.

XC Cross-country. "Going XC" means not intending to land close to the launch site.

Index

A
Aerobatics (acro) 46, 48, 49, 58
Ailerons 40
Airfoil 11

Altimeter 30, 31

B
Birds 6, 7, 60
Brakes 21, 22, 42, 47

C
Canopy 11, 17, 20, 21, 23,
   32, 42, 43, 47-50
Carabiners 19, 21
Carbon-fiber 40, 41
Cells 11, 20, 23, 42, 43
Cockpit 30, 31, 39
Competition hang gliders 36, 37
Competition paragliders 42, 43
Control bar 18, 23, 29, 61
Control frame 18, 19, 23, 30
Control lines 21, 29
Cross-country racing 45, 46, 47

D
Drag 27, 28, 41

F
Flying suit 28
Framework 7, 20
Free flight 7, 57

G
Gain-of-height 52, 53
GPS (Global Positioning System)
   30, 31, 47

H
Hang point 19
Harness 19, 20, 21, 27, 30, 31,
   32, 33, 40, 43
Hot air balloons 59

K
Keel 18, 19

L
Landing accuracy (paragliding)
   46, 47
Landing protection 33
Launching 23
Leading edge 14
Lilienthal, Otto 8, 9
Looping 48, 49, 59

M
Mount Everest 56, 57, 59

P
Pitch 16, 17

R
Radio 31
Ram-air effect 20
Ram-air parachute 11
Rescue parachute 32
Rigid hang gliders 40, 41, 53
Risers 21, 23
Rogallo gliders 10
Roll 16, 17, 22

S
Skiing 50, 51
Smoke trails/flares 22, 49

Spars 41
Speed arms 28
Speed flying 46, 50, 51
Speed gliding 51
Swift hang gliders 38, 39

T
Thermals 15, 32, 60
Trailing edge 14, 15, 21
Training hang gliders 36
Training paragliders 42, 43
Trim speed 22
Two-seat paraglider (tandem)
   56, 57

U
UV rays 27, 29

V
Variometer 30, 31, 61

W
Weight-shift control 16
Windchill 26
Wing collapse 42, 43
Wing-over 49
Wright brothers 10, 11

Y
Yaw 16, 17

About the Author

Noel Whittall started flying in 1973, with a hang glider he built himself. He has been flying all over the world ever since, in competitions and just for fun. These days Noel is best known for being the father of Rob Whittall, the first pilot ever to win world championships in both hang gliding and paragliding.